James R Bower

United States of America, States, Capitals and More

James R. Bower

Copyright © 2023 James R. Bower

All rights reserved. No part of this book may be reproduced or transmitted in any form or by any means, electronic or mechanical, including photocopying, recording or by any information storage and retrieval system without permission in writing from the publisher.

Average Dog Publishing–Deer Park, TX
Paperback ISBN: 978-1-7337590-6-9
Hardcover ISBN: 978-1-7337590-7-6
Library of Congress Control Number: 2023901665
Title: *United States of America, States, Capitals and More*
Author: James R. Bower
Paperback | 2023
Hardcover | 2023

Acknowledgements

In appreciation of my brother Ronald L. Bower for his idea's, encouragement and being my proof-reader.

INDEX

UNITED STATES MAP	1
1 DELAWARE	2
2 PENNSYLVANIA	5
3 NEW JERSEY	8
4 GEORGIA	11
5 CONNECTICUT	14
6 MASSACHUSETTS	17
7 MARYLAND	20
8 SOUTH CAROLINA	23
9 NEW HAMPSHIRE	26
10 VIRGINIA	29
11 NEW YORK	32
12 NORTH CAROLINA	35
13 RHODE ISLAND	38
14 VERMONT	41
15 KENTUCKY	44
16 TENNESSEE	47
17 OHIO	50

18 LOUISIANA	53
19 INDIANA	56
20 MISSISSIPPI	58
21 ILLINOIS	61
22 ALABAMA	64
23 MAINE	67
24 MISSOURI	70
25 ARKANSAS	73
26 MICHIGAN	76
27 FLORIDA	79
28 TEXAS	82
29 IOWA	85
30 WISCONSON	87
31 CALIFORNIA	89
32 MINNESOTA	92
33 OREGON	94
34 KANSAS	97
35 WEST VIRGINIA	100
36 NEVADA	103

37 NEBRASKA	106
38 COLORADO	109
39 NORTH DAKOTA	112
40 SOUTH DAKOTA	115
41 MONTANA	118
42 WASHINGTON	121
43 IDAHO	124
44 WYOMING	127
45 UTAH	130
46 OKLAHOMA	133
47 NEW MEXICO	136
48 ARIZONA	139
49 ALASKA	142
50 HAWAII	145
COLONIES	148
CONFEDERACY	152

UNITED STATES

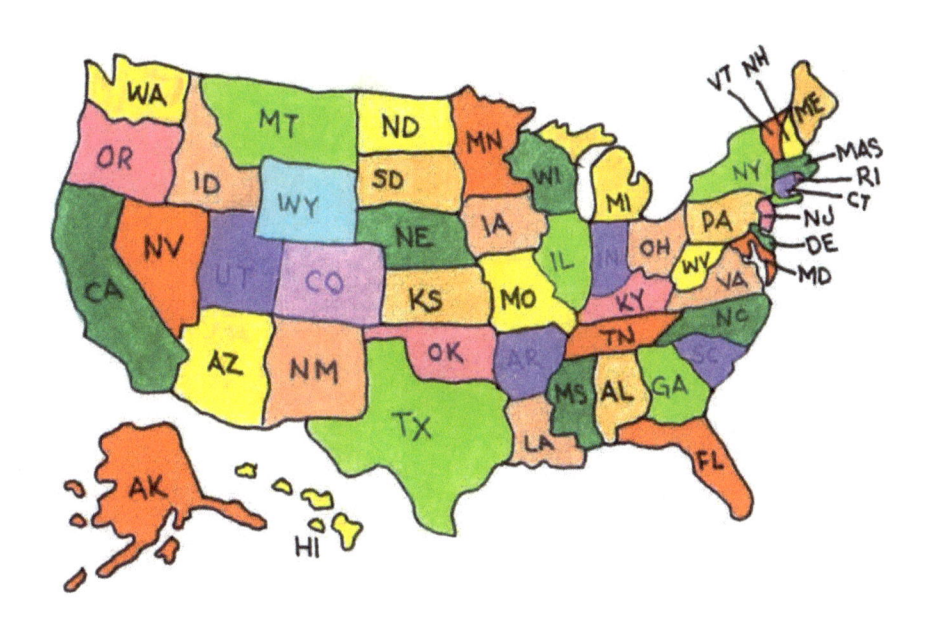

DELAWARE

1ST STATE

FLAG

CAPITAL - DOVER

SINCE - 1777

RATIFIED TO THE UNION - DEC. 7, 1787

FLOWER

PEACH BLOSSOM

BIRD

DELAWARE BLUE HEN

MAMMAL
GREY FOX

BUTTERFLY — EASTERN TIGER SWALLOWTAIL

FISH — WEAKFISH

INSECT — 7 SPOTTED LADYBUG

TREE — AMERICAN HOLLY

MAMMAL — GREY FOX

FLOWER — PEACH BLOSSOM

BIRD — DELAWARE BLUE HEN

PENNSYLVANIA

2ND STATE

FLAG

CAPITAL - HARRISBURG

SINCE - 1812

RATTIFIED TO THE UNION - DEC. 12, 1787

FLOWER

MOUNTAIN LAUREL

BIRD

RUFFED GROUSE

MAMMAL

WHITE-TAILED DEER

AMPHIBIAN - EASTERN HELLBINDER

DOG BREED - GREAT DANE

FISH - BROOK TROUT

INSECT - FIREFLY

TREE - EASTERN HEMLOCK

FLOWER - MOUNTAIN LAUREL

MAMMAL - WHITE-TAILED DEER

BIRD - RUFFED GROUSE

NEW JERSEY

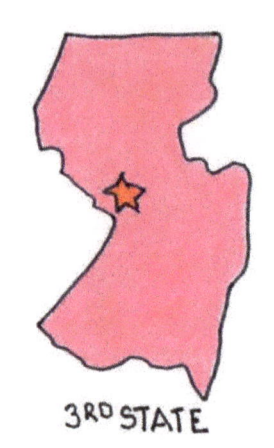

3RD STATE

FLAG

CAPITAL- TRENTON

SINCE- 1784

RATIFIED TO THE UNION- DEC. 18, 1787

FLOWER
NORTHERN HIGHBUSH BLUEBERRY

BIRD
EASTERN GOLDFINCH

MAMMAL
HORSE

FLOWER – NORTHERN HIGHBUSH BLUEBERRY

REPTILE – BOG TURTLE

TREE – DOGWOOD

DOG – SEEING EYE DOG

FISH – BROOK TROUT

INSECT – EUROPEAN HONEY BEE

BIRD – EASTERN GOLDFINCH

MAMMAL – HORSE

GEORGIA

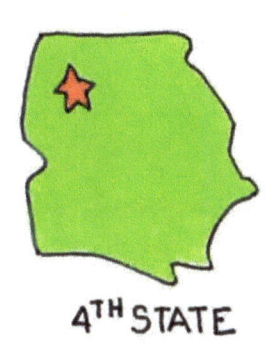

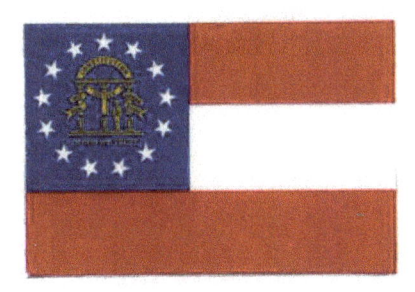

4TH STATE

FLAG

CAPITAL - ATLANTA

SINCE - 1868

RATIFIED TO THE UNION - JAN. 2, 1788

11

FLOWER
CHEROKEE ROSE

BIRD
BROWN THRASHER

MAMMAL
WHITE-TAILED DEER

DOG- ADOPTABLE DOG

FISH- LARGMOUTH BASS

INSECT- HONEYBEE

MAMMAL- WHITE-TAILED DEER, RIGHT WHALE

REPTILE- GOPHER TORTOISE

AMPHIBIAN- AMERICAN GREEN TREE FROG

FLOWER- CHEROKEE ROSE

BIRD- BROWN THRASHER

TREE- LIVE OAK

CONNECTICUT

5TH STATE

FLAG

CAPITAL - HARTFORD

SINCE - 1875

RATIFIED TO THE UNION - JAN. 7, 1788

FLOWER
MOUNTAIN LAUREL

BIRD
AMERICAN ROBIN

MAMMAL - SPERM WHALE
SHELL - EASTERN OYSTER
INSECT - PRAYING MANTIS
FISH - AMERICAN SHAD
TREE - WHITE OAK
BIRD - AMERICAN ROBIN
FLOWER - MOUNTAIN LAUREL

MASSACHUSETTS

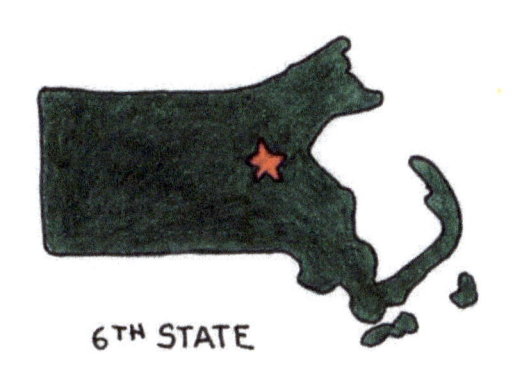

6TH STATE

FLAG

CAPITAL – BOSTON

SINCE – 1630

RATIFIED TO THE UNION – FEB. 6, 1788

FLOWER
MAYFLOWER

BIRD
BLACK-CAPPED CHICKADEE

MAMMAL

MORGAN HORSE

INSECT - LADYBUG

MAMMAL - TABBY CAT, BOSTON TERRIER, MORGAN HORSE, AND RIGHT WHALE

REPTILE - GARTER SNAKE

TREE - AMERICAN ELM

BIRD - BLACK-CAPPED CHICKADEE

FLOWER - MAYFLOWER

MARYLAND

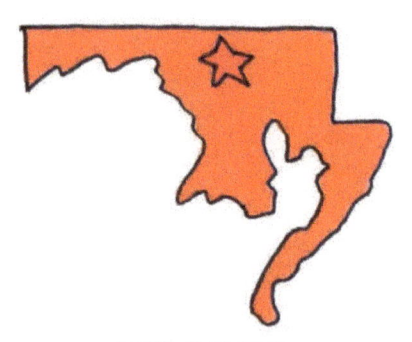

7TH STATE

FLAG

CAPITAL - ANNAPOLIS

SINCE - 1694

RATIFIED TO THE UNION - APRIL 28, 1788

FLOWER
BLACK-EYED SUSAN

BIRD
BALTIMORE ORIOLE

MAMMAL
THOROUGHBRED HORSE

BIRD - BALTIMORE ORIOLE

BUTTERELY - BALTIMORE CHECKERSPOT BUTTERFLY

CRUSTACEAN - BLUE CRAB

FISH - ROCKFISH

FLOWER - BLACK-EYED SUSAN

INSECT - BALTIMORE CHECKERSPOT

MAMMAL - CALICO CAT, CHESAPEAK BAY RETRIEVER, THOROUGHBRED HORSE

REPTILE - DIAMONDBACK TERRAPIN

TREE - WHITE OAK

SOUTH CAROLINA

8TH STATE

FLAG

CAPITAL - COLUMBIA

SINCE - 1786

RATIFIED TO THE UNION - MAY 23, 1788

FLOWER
YELLOW JESSAMINE

BIRD
CAROLINA WREN

MAMMAL
WHITE-TAILED DEER

AMPHIBIAN - SALAMANDER

BUTTERFLY - EASTERN TIGER SWALLOWTAIL

DOG BREED - BOYKIN SPANIEL

FISH - STRIPED BASS

INSECT - CAROLINA MANTIS

REPTILE - LOGGERHEAD SEA TURTLE

TREE - SABAL PALMETTO

FLOWER - YELLOW JESSAMINE

BIRD - CAROLINA WREN

MAMMAL - WHITE-TAILED DEER

NEW HAMPSHIRE

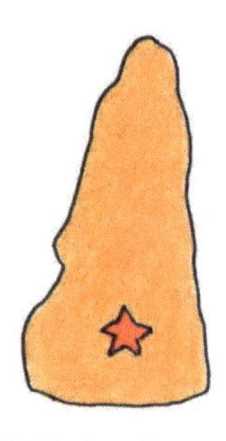

9TH STATE

FLAG

CAPITAL- CONCORD

SINCE- 1808

RATIFIED-TO THE UNION- JUNE 21, 1788

FLOWER
PURPLE LILAC

BIRD
PURPLE FINCH

MAMMAL

WHITE-TAILED DEER

AMPHIBIAN- RED SPOTTED NEWT

BUTTERFLY- KARNER BLUE

DOG BREED- CHINOOK

FISH- FRESHWATER- BROOK TROUT
SALTWATER- STRIPED BASS

INSECT- LADYBUG

TREE- WHITE BIRCH

FLOWER- PURPLE LILAC

MAMMAL- WHITE-TAILED DEER

BIRD- PURPLE FINCH

VIRGINA

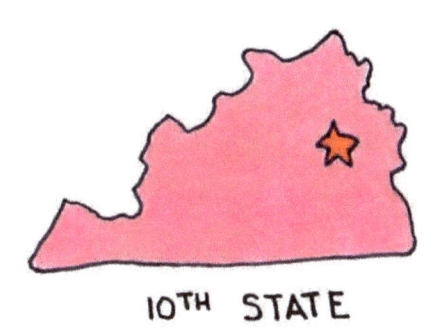

10TH STATE

FLAG

CAPITAL - RICHMOND

SINCE - 1780

RATIFIED TO THE UNION - JUNE 25, 1788

FLOWER
FLOWERING DOGWOOD

BIRD
CARDINAL

BIRD - CARDINAL

BUTTERFLY - TIGER SWALLOWTAIL

DOG BREED - AMERICAN FOXHOUND

FISH - BROOK TROUT - STRIPED BASS

FLOWER - FLOWERING DOGWOOD

INSECT - TIGER SWALLOWTAIL BUTTERFLY

TREE - FLOWERING DOGWOOD

NEW YORK

11TH STATE

FLAG

CAPITAL - ALBANY

SINCE - 1797

RATIFIED TO THE UNION - JULY 26, 1788

FLOWER
ROSE

BIRD
EASTERN BLUEBIRD

MAMMAL

NORTH AMERICAN BEAVER

BIRD - EASTERN BLUEBIRD

FISH - BROOK TROUT - STRIPED BASS

FLOWER - ROSE

INSECT - NINE SPOTTED LADYBUG

MAMMAL - NORTH AMERICAN BEAVER

REPTILE - COMMON SNAPPING TURTLE

TREE - SURGAR MAPLE

NORTH CAROLINA

12TH STATE

FLAG

CAPITAL - RALEIGH

SINCE - 1792

RATIFIED TO THE UNION - NOV, 21, 1798

FLOWER
FLOWERING DOGWOOD

BIRD
CARDINAL

MAMMAL
EASTERN GRAY SQUIRREL

BIRD - CARDINAL

BUTTERFLY - EASTERN TIGER SWALLOWTAIL

FISH - RED DRUM

FLOWER - FLOWERING DOGWOOD

INSECT - WESTERN HONEY BEE

MAMMAL - EASTERN GRAY SQUIRREL

MARSUPIAL - VIRGINIA OPOSSUM

REPTILE - EASTERN BOX TURTLE

TREE - PINE

RHODE ISLAND

13TH STATE

FLAG

CAPITAL - PROVIDENCE

SINCE - 1900

RATIFIED TO THE UNION - MAY 29, 1790

FLOWER
VIOLET

MAMMAL
MORGAN HORSE

BIRD

BIRD - RHODE ISLAND RED CHICKEN

FISH - STRIPED BASS

FLOWER - VIOLET

INSECT - AMERICAN BURYING BEATLE

MAMMAL - MORGAN HORSE

REPTILE - PAINTED TURTLE

TREE - RED MAPLE

VERMONT

14TH STATE

FLAG

CAPITAL – MONTPELIER

SINCE – 1805

ADMITTED TO THE UNION – MARCH 4, 1791

FLOWER

RED CLOVER

BIRD

HERMIT THRUST

MAMMAL
MORGAN HORSE

AMPHIBIAN – NORTHERN LEOPARD FROG

BIRD – HERMIT THRUST

FISH – BROOK TROUT

FLOWER – RED CLOVER

INSECT – WESTERN HONEY BEE

MAMMAL – MORGAN HORSE

REPTILE – PAINTED TURTLE

TREE – SUGER MAPLE

KENTUCKY

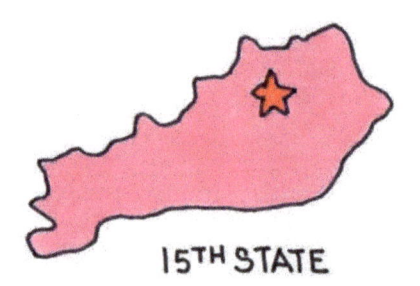

15TH STATE

FLAG

CAPITAL - FRANKFORT

SINCE - 1792

ADMITTED TO THE UNION - JUNE 1, 1792

FLOWER
GOLDENROD

BIRD
CARDINAL

MAMMAL
GRAY SQUIRREL

BIRD - CARDINAL

BUTTERFLY - VICEROY BUTTERFLY

MAMMAL - GRAY SQUIRREL

FISH - KENTUCKY SPOTTED BASS

FLOWER - GOLDENROD

HORSE BREED - THOUROUGHBRED

INSECT - WESTERN HONEYBEE

TREE - TULIP POPLAR

TENNESSEE

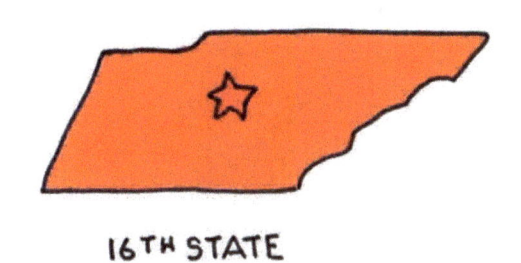

16TH STATE

FLAG

CAPITAL - NASHVILLE

SINCE - 1826

ADMITTED TO THE UNION - JUNE 1, 1798

FLOWER
IRIS

BIRD
MOCKING BIRD

MAMMAL
TENNESSEE WALKING HORSE

AMPHIBIAN- TENNESSEE CAVE SALAMANDER

BIRD- MOCKING BIRD- BOBWHITE QUAIL

BUTTERFLY- ZEBRA SWALLOWTAIL

FISH- CHANNEL CATFISH, SMALLMOUTH BASS

FLOWER- IRIS, PASSION FLOWER, TENNESSEE ECHINCEA

INSECT- FIREFLY, LADY BEETLE, HONEY BEE

MAMMAL- TENNESSEE WALKING HORSE, RACCOON

REPTILE- EASTERN BOX TURTLE

TREE- TULIP POPLAR, EASTERN RED CIDAR

OHIO

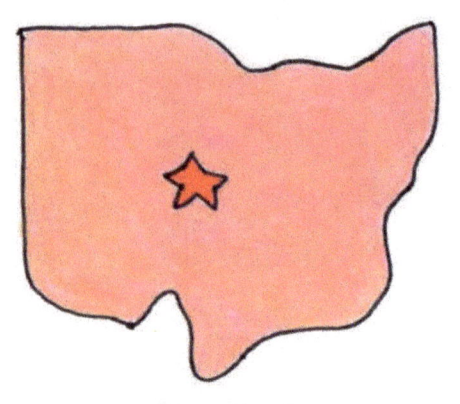

17TH STATE

FLAG

CAPITAL - COLUMBUS

SINCE - 1816

ADMITTED TO THE UNION - MARCH 1, 1803

FLOWER
RED CARNATION

BIRD
CARDINAL

MAMMAL
WHITE-TAILED DEER

AMPHIBIAN - SPOTTED SALAMANDER

BIRD - CARDINAL

FLOWER - RED CARNATION

INSECT - LADYBUG

MAMMAL - WHITE TAILED DEER

REPTILE - BLACK RACER SNAKE

TREE - BUCKEYE

LOUISIANA

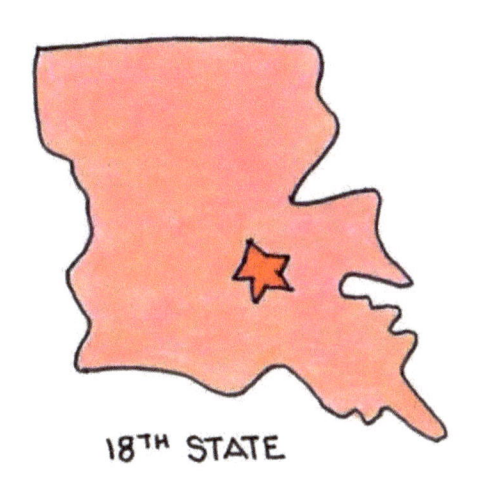

18TH STATE

FLAG

CAPITAL- BATON ROUGE

SINCE - 1880

ADMITTED TO THE UNION - APRIL 30, 1812

FLOWER
MAGNOLIA

BIRD
BROWN PELICAN

MAMMAL
BLACK BEAR

BIRD- BROWN PELICAN

DOG BREED- CATAHOULA LEAPARD DOG

FISH- WHITE PERCH

FLOWER- MAGNOLIA

INSECT- HONEYBEE

MAMMAL- BLACK BEAR

REPTILE- ALLIGATOR

TREE- BALD CYPRESS

INDIANA

19TH STATE

FLAG

CAPITAL- INDIANAPOLIS

SINCE- 1825

ADMITTED TO THE UNION- DEC. 11, 1816

FLOWER
PEONY

BIRD
CARDINAL

BIRD- CARDINAL
FLOWER- PEONY
INSECT- FIREFLY
TREE- TULIP TREE

MISSISSIPPI

20TH STATE

FLAG

CAPITAL- JACKSON

SINCE- 1821

ADMITTED TO THE UNION- DEC. 10, 1817

FLOWER
MAGNOLIA

BIRD
NORTHERN MOCKING BIRD

MAMMAL

WHITE-TAILED DEER

BIRD- NORTHERN MOCKING BIRD

BUTTERFLY- SPICEBUSH SWALLOWTAIL

FISH- LARGEMOUTH BASS

FLOWER- MAGNOLIA

INSECT- WESTERN HONEYBEE

MAMMAL- WHITE-TAILED DEER

REPTILE- AMERICAN ALLIGATOR

TREE- SOUTHERN MAGNOLIA

ILLINOIS

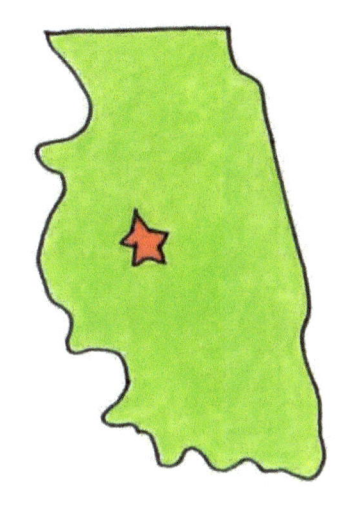

21ST STATE

FLAG

CAPITAL - SPRINGFIELD

SINCE - 1837

ADMITTED TO THE UNION - DEC. 3, 1818

FLOWER
VIOLET

BIRD
NORTHERN CARDINAL

MAMMAL
WHITE-TAILED DEER

ANPHIBIAN- EASTERN TIGER SALAMANDER

BIRD- NORTHERN CARDINAL

BUTTERFLY- MONARCH BUTTERFLY

FISH- BLUEGILL

FLOWER- VIOLET

GRASS- BIG BLUESTEM

MAMMAL- WHITE-TAILED DEER

REPTILE- PAINTED TURTLE

TREE- WHITE OAK

ALABAMA

22ND STATE

FLAG

CAPITAL- MONTGOMERY

SINCE- 1846

ADMITTED TO THE UNION- DEC. 14, 1819

FLOWER
CAMELLIA

BIRD
YELLOW HAMMER

MAMMAL
AMERICAN BLACK BEAR

ANPHIBIAN- RED HILLS SALAMANDER

BIRD- YELLOWHAMMER, WILD TURKEY

BUTTERFLY- EASTERN TIGER SWALLOWTAIL

FISH- LARGEMOUTH BASS, FIGHTING TARPON

FLOWER- CAMELLIA, OAK LEAF, HYDRANGEA

HORSE BREED- RACKING HORSE

INSECT- MONARCH BUTTERFLY

MAMMAL- AMERICAN BLACK BEAR

REPTILE- ALABAMA RED-BELLIED TURTLE

TREE- LONGLEAF PINE

MAINE

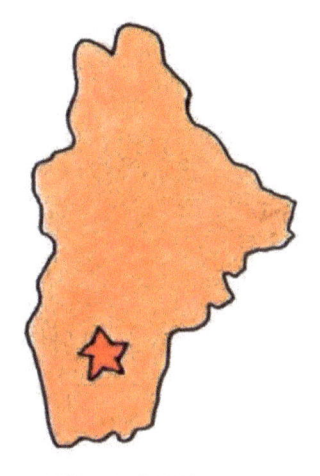

23RD STATE

FLAG

CAPITAL- AUGUSTA

SINCE- 1832

AMITTED TO THE UNION- MARCH 15, 1820

FLOWER

WHITE PINE CONE

BIRD

BLACK-CAPPED CHICKADEE

MAMMAL

MOOSE

BIRD - BLACK-CAPPED CHICKADEE

CAT BREED - MAINE COON

CRUSTACEAN - LOBSTER

FISH - LANDLOCKED ATLANTIC SALMON

FLOWER - WHITE PINE CONE

MAMMAL - MOOSE

MISSOURI

24TH STATE

FLAG

CAPITAL - JEFFERSON CITY

SINCE - 1826

ADMITTED TO THE UNION - AUG. 10, 1821

FLOWER
WHITE HAWTHORN

BIRD
EASTERN BLUEBIRD

MAMMAL
MISSOURI MULE

AMPHIBIAN- AMERICAN BULLFROG

BIRD- EASTERN BLUEBIRD

FISH- CHANNEL CATFISH

FLOWER- WHITE HAWTHORN

GRASS- BIG BLUESTEM

HORSE BREED- MISSOURI FOX TROTTER

INSECT- HONEY BEE

MAMMAL- MISSOURI MULE

TREE- FLOWERING DOGWOOD

ARKANSAS

25TH STATE

FLAG

CAPITAL- LITTLE ROCK

SINCE- 1821

ADMITTED TO THE UNION- JUNE 15, 1836

FLOWER
APPLE BLOSSOM

BIRD
MOCKING BIRD

MAMMAL
WHITE-TAILED DEER

BIRD - MOCKINGBIRD

BUTTERFLY - DIANA FRITILLARY

FLOWER - APPLE BLOSSOM

INSECT - WESTERN HONEYBEE

MAMMAL - WHITE-TAILED DEER

TREE - PINE TREE

MICHIGAN

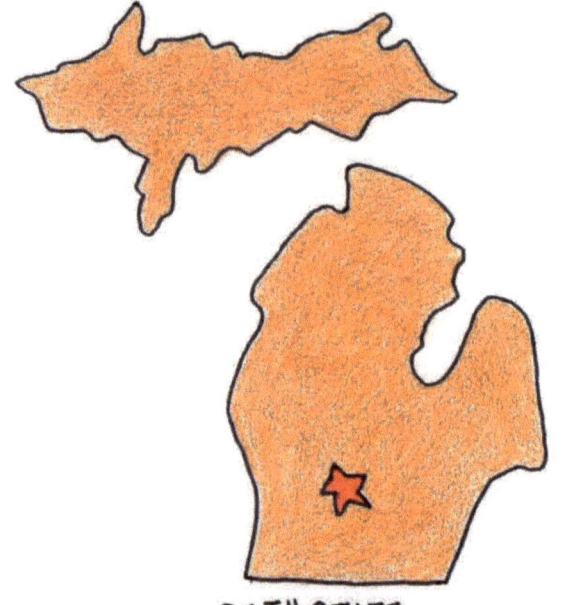

26TH STATE

FLAG

CAPITAL - LANSING

SINCE - 1847

ADMITTED TO THE UNION - JAN. 26, 1837

76

FLOWER
APPLE BLOSSOM

BIRD
AMERICAN ROBIN

MAMMAL

WOLVERINE

BIRD - AMERICAN ROBIN

FISH - BROOK TROUT

FLOWER - APPLE BLOSSOM, DWARF LAKE IRIS

MAMMAL - WOLVERINE, WHITE-TAILED DEER

REPTILE - PAINTED TURTLE

TREE - EASTERN WHITE PINE

FLORIDA

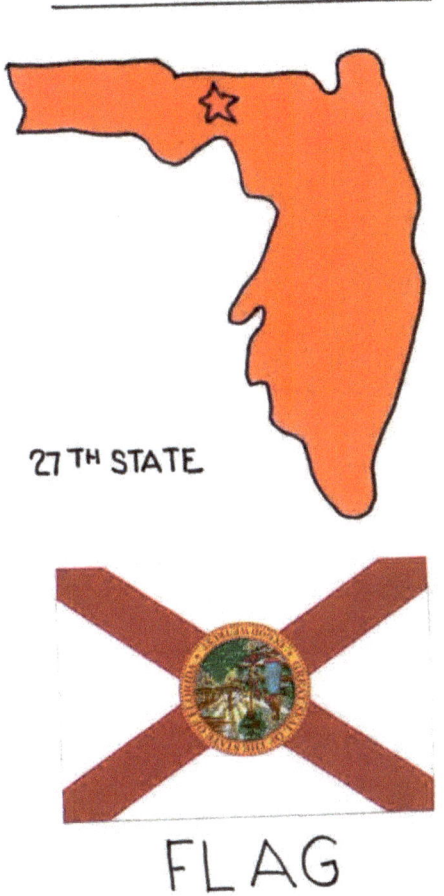

27TH STATE

FLAG

CAPITAL- TALLAHASSEE

SINCE- 1824

ADMITTED TO THE UNION- MARCH 3, 1845

FLOWER
ORANGE BLOSSOM

BIRD
NORTHERN MOCKING BIRD

MAMMAL
FLORIDA PANTHER

AMPHIBIAN - BARKING TREE FROG

BIRD - NORTHERN MOCKING BIRD

FISH - FLORIDA LARGEMOUTH BASS, ATLANTIC SAILFISH

FLOWER - ORANGE BLOSSOM

INSECT - ZEBRA LONGWING

MAMMAL - FLORIDA PANTHER, MANATEE, BOTTLE NOSED DOLPHIN, FLORIDA CRACKER HORSE

REPTILE - AMERICAN ALLIGATOR, LOGGERHEAD TURTLE, GOLPHER TORTOISE

TREE - SABAL PAMETTO

TEXAS

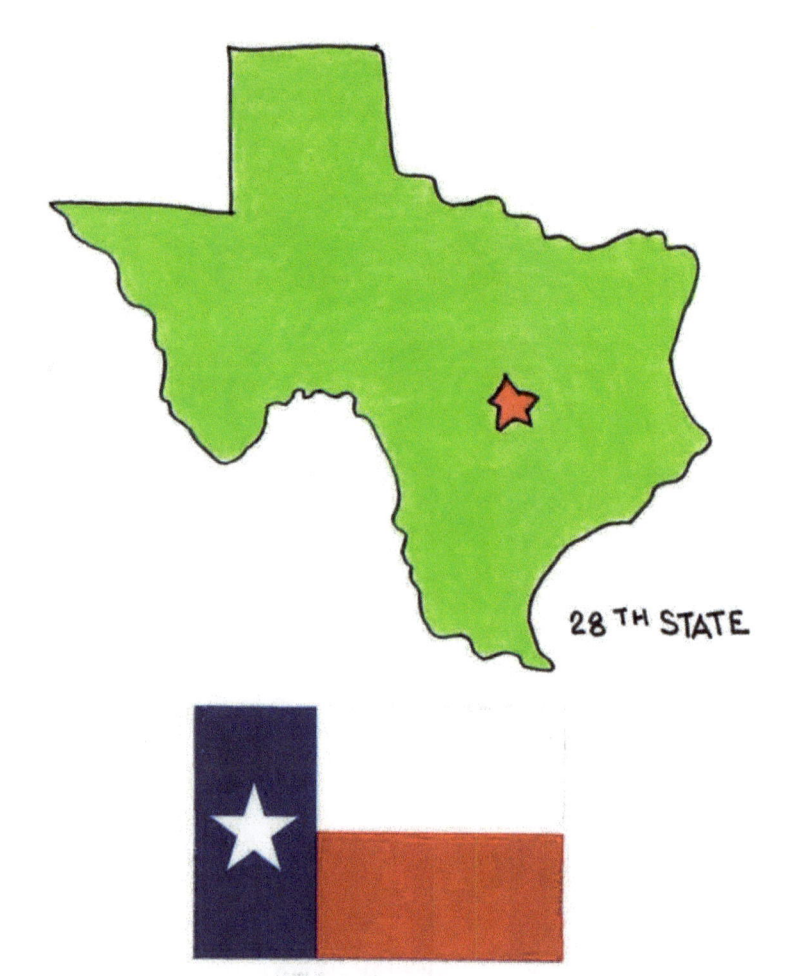

28TH STATE

FLAG

CAPITAL - AUSTIN

SINCE - 1839

ADMITTED TO THE UNION - DEC. 29, 1845

FLOWER
BLUEBONNET

BIRD
EASTERN MOCKINGBIRD

MAMMAL
TEXAS LONGHORN

BIRD- NORTHERN MOCKINGBIRD

FISH- GUADALUPE BASS

FLOWER- BLUEBONNET

INSECT- MONARCH BUTTERFLY

MAMMAL- TEXAS LONGHORN, NINE-BANDED ARMADILLO

MUSHROOM- TEXAS STAR

REPTILE- TEXAS HORNED LIZARD

TREE- PECAN

IOWIA

29TH STATE

FLAG

CAPITAL- DES MOINES

SINCE- 1857

ADMITTED TO THE UNION- DEC. 28, 1846

FLOWER
PRAIRE ROSE

BIRD
EASTERN GOLDFINCH

BIRD- EASTERN GOLDFINCH
FLOWER- PRAIRIE ROSE
TREE- BUR OAK

WISCONSIN

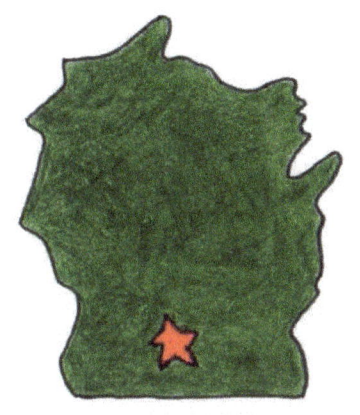

30TH STATE

FLAG

CAPITAL- MADISON

SINCE- 1838

ADMITTED TO THE UNION- MAY 29, 1848

FLOWER
WOOD VIOLET

BIRD
AMERICAN ROBIN

BIRD - AMERICAN ROBIN

FISH - MUSKELLUNGE

FLOWER - WOOD VIOLET

INSECT - WESTERN HONEYBEE

TREE - SUGAR MAPLE

CALIFORNIA

31ST STATE

FLAG

CAPITAL- SACRAMENTO

SINCE- 1854

ADMITTED TO THE UNION- SEPT. 9, 1850

FLOWER
CALIFORNIA POPPY

BIRD
CALIFORNIA QUAIL

MAMMAL
CALIFORNIA GRIZZLY BEAR

AMPHIBEAN- CALIFORNIA RED LEGGED FROG

BIRD- CALIFORNIA QUAIL

FISH- GOLDEN TROUT, GARIBALDI

FLOWER- CALIFORNIA POPPY

GRASS- PURPLE NEEDLE GRASS

INSECT- CALIFORNIA DOGFACE BUTTERFLY

MAMMAL- CALIFORNIA GRIZZLY BEAR, GREY WHALE

REPTLE- DESERT TORTOISE

TREE- COAST REDWOOD, GIANT SEQUOIA

MINNESOTA

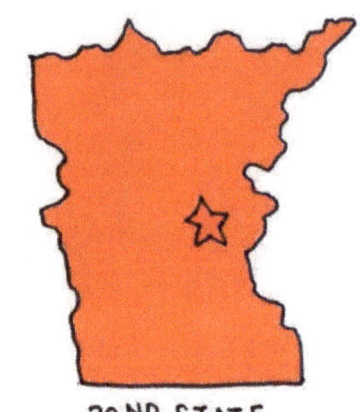

32ND STATE

FLAG

CAPITAL- SAINT PAUL

SINCE- 1849

ADMITTED TO THE UNION- MAY 11, 1858

FLOWER
PINK AND WHITE LADY SLIPPER

BIRD
COMMON LOON

BIRD- COMMON LOON

BUTTERFLY- MONARCH

FISH- WALLEYE

FLOWER- PINK AND WHITE LADY SLIPPER

MUSHROOM- COMMON MOREL

TREE- NORWAY PINE

OREGON

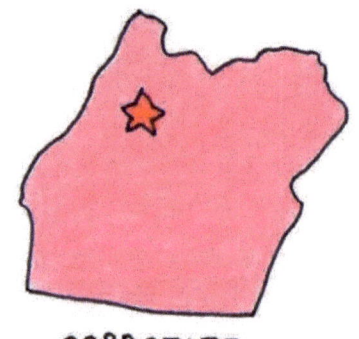

33RD STATE

STATE OF OREGON
1859

FLAG

CAPITAL- SALEM

SINCE- 1855

ADMITTED TO THE UNION- FEB. 14, 1859

FLOWER
OREGON GRAPE

BIRD
WESTERN MEADOWLARK

MAMMAL

AMERICAN BEAVER

BIRD- WESTERN MEADOWLARK

CRUSTACEAN- DUNGENESS CRAB

FISH- CHINOOK SALMON

FLOWER- OREGON GRAPE

GRASS- BLUEBUNCH WHEATGRASS

INSECT- OREGON SWALLOWTAIL

MAMMAL- AMERICAN BEAVER

MUSHROOM- PACIFIC GOLDEN CHANTERELLE

TREE- DOUGLUS FIR

KANSAS

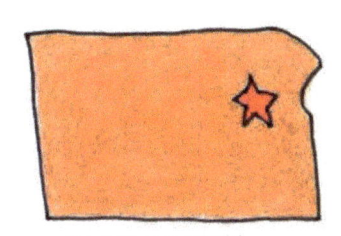

34TH STATE

FLAG

CAPITAL - TOPEKA

SINCE - 1858

ADMITTED TO THE UNION - JAN. 29, 1861

FLOWER

WESTERN SUNFLOWER

BIRD

WESTERN MEADOWLARK

MAMMAL
AMERICAN BISON

ANPHIBEAN- BARRED TIGER SALAMANDER

BIRD- WESTERN MEADOWLARK

FLOWER- WILD SUNFLOWER

GRASS- LITTLE BLUESTEM

INSECT- WESTERN HONEYBEE

MAMMAL- AMERICAN BISON

REPTILE- ORNATE BOX TURTLE

TREE- PLAINS COTTONWOOD

WEST VIRGINIA

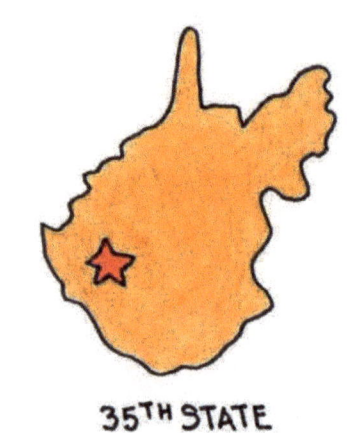

35TH STATE

FLAG

CAPITAL - CHARLSTON

SINCE - 1885

ADMITTED TO THE UNION - JUNE 20, 1863

FLOWER

RHODODENDRON

BIRD

NORTHERN CARDINAL

MAMMAL
BLACK BEAR

BIRD- NORTHERN CARDINAL

BUTTERFLY- MONARCH BUTTERFLY

FISH- BROOK TROUT

FLOWER- RHODODENDRON

INSECT- WESTERN HONEYBEE

MAMMAL- BLACK BEAR

REPTILE- TIMBER RATTLESNAKE

TREE- SUGAR MAPLE

NEVADA

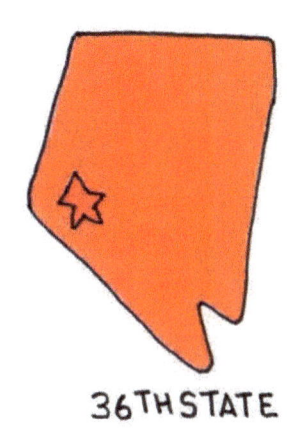

36TH STATE

FLAG

CAPITAL- CARSON CITY

SINCE- 1861

ADMITTED TO THE UNION- OCTOBER 31, 1864

FLOWER

SAGEBRUSH

BIRD

MOUNTAIN BLUEBIRD

MAMMAL

DESERT BIGHORN SHEEP

BIRD- MOUNTAIN BLUEBIRD

FISH- LAHORTAN CUTTHROAT TROUT

FLOWER- SAGEBRUSH

GRASS- INDIAN RICE GRASS

INSECT- VIVID DANCER DAMSELFLY

MAMMAL- DESERT BIGHORN SHEEP

REPTILE- DESERT TORTOISE

TREE- BRISTLECONE PINE, SINGLE LEAF PINON

NEBRASKA

37TH STATE

FLAG

CAPITAL- LINCOLN

SINCE- 1867

ADMITTED TO THE UNION- MARCH 1, 1867

FLOWER

TALL GOLDENROD

BIRD

WESTERN MEADOWLARK

MAMMAL

WHITE-TAILED DEER

BIRD- WESTERN MEADOWLARK
FISH- CHANNEL CATFISH
FLOWER- TALL GOLDENROD
GRASS- LITTLE BLUESTEM
INSECT- WESTERN HONEYBEE
MAMMAL- WHITE-TAILED DEER
TREE- EASTERN COTTONWOOD

COLORADO

38TH STATE

FLAG

CAPITAL - DENVER

SINCE - 1867

ADMITTED TO THE UNION - AUGUST 1, 1876

FLOWER
ROCKY MOUNTAIN COLUMBINE

BIRD
LARK BUNTING

MAMMAL

ROCKY MOUNTAIN BIGHORN SHEEP

AMPHIBIAN- WESTERN TIGER SALAMANDER

BIRD- LARK BUNTING

CACTUS- CLARET CUP CACTUS

FISH- GREENBACK CUTTHROAT TROUT

FLOWER- ROCKY MOUNTAIN COLUMBINE

GRASS- BLUE GRAMA GRASS

INSECT- COLORADO HAIRSTREAK

MAMMAL- ROCKY MOUNTAIN BIGHORN SHEEP

PET- COLORADO SHELTER PETS

REPTILE- WESTERN PAINTED TURTLE

TREE- COLORADO BLUE SPRUCE

NORTH DAKOTA

39TH STATE

FLAG

CAPITAL - BISMARK

SINCE - 1889

ADMITTED TO THE UNION - NOV. 2, 1889

FLOWER
WILD PRAIRE ROSE

BIRD
WESTERN MEADOWLARK

MAMMAL
NAKOTA HORSE

BIRD - WESTERN MEADOWLARK

FISH - NORTHERN PIKE

FLOWER - WILD PRAIRIE ROSE

GRASS - WESTERN WHEAT GRASS

INSECT - WESTERN HONEYBEE

MAMMAL - NAKOTA HORSE

TREE - AMERICAN ELM

SOUTH DAKOTA

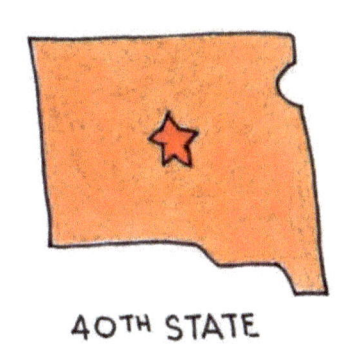

40TH STATE

FLAG

CAPITAL- PIERRE

SINCE- 1889

ADMITTED TO THE UNION- NOV. 2, 1889

FLOWER
AMERICAN PASQUE FLOWER

BIRD
RING-NECKED PHEASANT

MAMMAL

COYOTE

BIRD - RING-NECKED PHEASANT

FISH - WALLEYE

FLOWER - AMERICAN PASQUE FLOWER

GRASS - WESTERN WHEATGRASS

INSECT - WESTERN HONEYBEE

MAMMAL - COYOTE

TREE - BLACK HILLS SPRUCE

MONTANA

41ST STATE

FLAG

CAPITAL - HELENA

SINCE - 1875

ADMITTED TO THE UNION - NOV. 8, 1889

FLOWER
BITTERROOT

BIRD
WESTERN MEADOWLARK

MAMMAL

GRIZZLEY BEAR

BIRD- WESTERN MEADOWLARK

BUTTERFLY- MOURNING CLOAK

FLOWER- BITTERROOT

MAMMAL- GRIZZLEY BEAR

TREE- PONDEROSA PINE

WASHINGTON

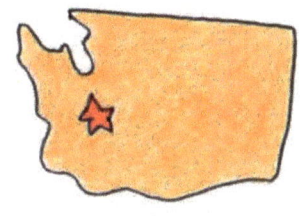

42ND STATE

FLAG

CAPITAL- OLYMPIA

SINCE- 1853

ADMITTED TO THE UNION- NOV. 11, 1889

FLOWER
RHODODENDRON

BIRD
AMERICAN GOLDFINCH

MAMMAL
OLYMPIC MARMOT

AMPHIBIAN- PACIFIC CHORUS FROG

BIRD- AMERICAN GOLDFINCH

FISH- STEELHEAD TROUT

FLOWER- RHODODENDRON

GRASS- BLUEBUNCH WHEATGRASS

INSECT- GREEN DARNER

MAMMAL- OLYMPIC MARMOT, ORCA

TREE- WESTERN HEMLOCK

IDAHO

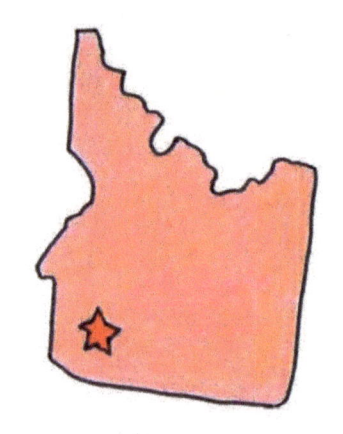

43RD STATE

FLAG

CAPITAL - BOISE

SINCE - 1865

ADMITTED TO THE UNION - JULY 3, 1890

FLOWER
SYRINGA

BIRD
MOUNTAIN BLUEBIRD

HORSE BREED
APPALOOSA

AMPHIBIAN- TIGER SALAMANDER

BIRD- MOUNTAIN BLUEBIRD

FISH- CUTTHROAT TROUT

FLOWER- SYRINGA

HORSE BREED- APPALOOSA

INSECT- MONARCH BUTTERFLY

TREE- WESTERN WHITE PINE

WYOMING

44TH STATE

FLAG

CAPITAL- CHEYENNE

SINCE- 1869

ADMITTED TO THE UNION- JULY 10, 1890

FLOWER

WYOMING INDIAN

BIRD

WESTERN MEADOWLARK

MAMMAL
AMERICAN BISON

BIRD - WESTERN MEADOWLARK

FISH - CUTTHROAT TROUT

FLOWER - WYOMING INDIAN

GRASS - WESTERN WHEATGRASS

MAMMAL - AMERICAN BISON

REPTILE - HORNED LIZARD

TREE - PLAINS COTTONWOOD

UTAH

45TH STATE

FLAG

CAPITAL- SALT LAKE CITY

SINCE- 1858

ADMITTED TO THE UNION- JAN. 4, 1896

FLOWER
SEGO LILY

BIRD
CALIFORNIA GULL

MAMMAL

ROCKY MOUNTAIN ELK

BIRD- CALIFORNIA GULL

FISH- BONNEVILLE CUTTHROAT TROUT

FLOWER- SEGO LILY

GRASS- INDIAN RICEGRASS

MAMMAL- ROCKY MOUNTAIN ELK

REPTILE- GILA MONSTER

TREE- QUAKING ASPEN

OKLAHOMA

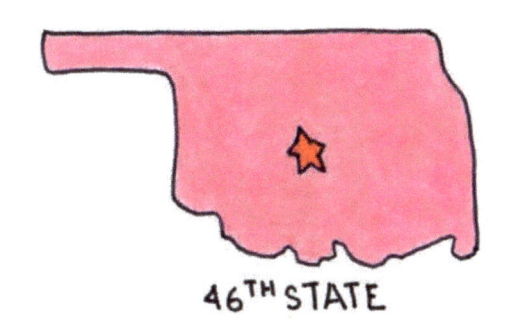

46TH STATE

FLAG

CAPITAL - OKLAHOMA CITY

SINCE - 1910

ADMITTED TO THE UNION - NOV. 16, 1907

FLOWER
OKLAHOMA ROSE

BIRD
SCISSOR-TAILED FLYCATCHER

MAMMAL

AMERICAN BISON

AMPHIBIAN- BULLFROG

BIRD- SCISSOR-TAILED FLYCATCHER

FISH- SAND BASS

FLOWER- OKLAHOMA ROSE, INDIAN BLANKET

GRASS- INDIAN GRASS

INSECT- EUROPEAN HONEYBEE

MAMMAL- AMERICAN BISON

REPTILE- MOUNTAIN BOOMER

TREE- REDBUD

NEW MEXICO

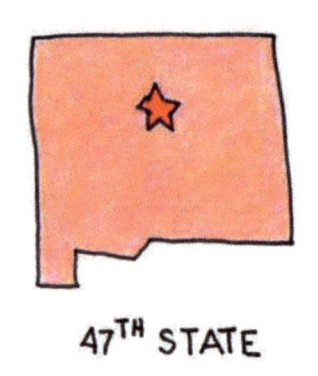

47TH STATE

FLAG

CAPITAL- SANTA FE

SINCE- 1610

ADMITTED TO THE UNION- JAN. 6, 1912

FLOWER
YUCCA

BIRD
GREATER ROADRUNNER

MAMMAL

AMERICAN BLACK BEAR

BIRD- GREATER ROADRUNNER

FISH- RIO GRAND CUTTHROAT TROUT

FLOWER- YUCCA

GRASS- BLUE GRAMA

INSECT- TARANTULA HAWK WASP

MAMMAL- AMERICAN BLACK BEAR

REPTILE- NEW MEXICO WHIPTAIL

TREE- TWO-NEEDLE PINON

ARIZONA

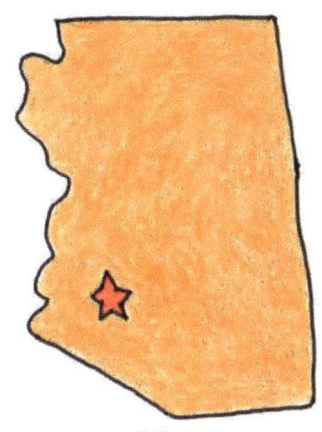

48TH STATE

FLAG

CAPITAL- PHOENIX

SINCE- 1889

ADMITTED TO THE UNION- FEB. 14, 1912

FLOWER

SAGUARO CACTUS BLOSSOM

BIRD

CACTUS WREN

MAMMAL
RINGTAIL

AMPHIBIAN- ARIZONA TREE FROG

BIRD- CACTUS WREN

BUTTERFLY- TWO-TAILED SWALLOWTAIL

FISH- APACHE TROUT

FLOWER- SAGUARO CACTUS BLOSSOM

MAMMAL- RINGTAIL

REPTILE- ARIZONA RIDGE-NOSED RATTLESNAKE

TREE- PALO VERDE

ALASKA

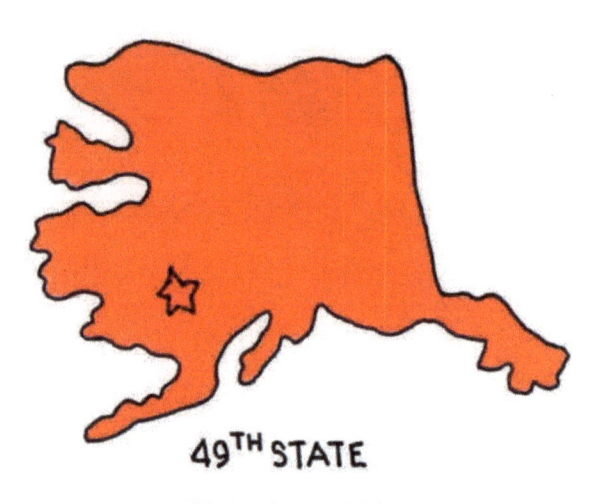

49TH STATE

FLAG

CAPITAL- JUNEAU

SINCE- 1906

ADMITTED TO THE UNION- JAN. 3, 1959

FLOWER

FORGET-ME-NOT

BIRD

WILLOW PTARMIGAM

MAMMAL

MOOSE

BIRD- WILLOW PTARMIGAM

DOG BREED- ALASKEN MALAMUTE

FISH- KING SALMON

FLOWER- FORGET-ME-NOT

INSECT- FOUR-SPOT SKIMMER DRAGONFLY

MAMMAL- MOOSE, BOWHEAD WHALE

TREE- SITKA SPRUCE

HAWAII

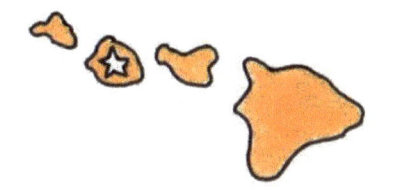

50TH STATE

FLAG

CAPITAL- HONOLULU

SINCE- 1845

ADMITTED TO THE UNION- AUG. 21, 1959

FLOWER
PUA ALOALO

BIRD
NENE

BIRD- NENE

FISH- HUMUHUMUNUKUNUKUAPUA'A

FLOWER- PUA ALOALO

INSECT- PUEELEHUA

TREE- KUKUI TREE

COLONIES

THE THIRTEEN BRITISH COLONIES WERE FOUNDED IN THE 17TH AND 18TH CENTURIES. THEY BEGAN FIGHTING THE REVOLUTIONARY WAR IN APRIL 1775 AND FORMED THE UNITED STATES OF AMERICA BY DECLARING FULL INDEPENDENCE IN JULY 1776. PRIOR TO DECLARING THEIR INDEPENDENCE THE THIRTEEN COLONIES WERE:

NEW HAMPSHIRE
MASSACHUSETTS
RHODE ISLAND
CONNECTICUT
NEW YORK
NEW JERSEY
PENNSYLVANIA
DELEWARE
MARYLAND
VIRGINIA
NORTH CAROLINA
SOUTH CAROLINA
GEORGIA

THE UNITED STATES DECLARATION OF INDEPENDENCE FORMALLY THE UNANIMOUS DECLARATION OF THE THIRTEEN UNITED STATES OF AMERICA, IS THE PRONOUNCEMENT ADOPTED BY THE SECOND CONTINENTAL CONGRESS MEETING IN PHILADELPHIA, PENNSYLVANIA, ON JULY 4, 1776. ENACTED DURING THE AMERICAN REVOLUTION, THE DECLARATION EXPLAINS WHY THE THIRTEEN COLONIES AT WAR WITH THE KINGDOM OF GREAT BRITAIN REGARDED THEMSELVES AS THIRTEEN INDEPENDENT SOVEREIGN STATES, NO LONGER UNDER BRITISH RULE. WITH THE DECLARATION, THESE NEW STATES TOOK A FIRST STEP IN FORMING THE UNITED STATES OF AMERICA. THE DECLARATION WAS SIGNED BY 56 REPRESENTATIVES FROM:

NEW HAMPSHIRE: JOSIAH BARTETT, WILLIAM WHIPPLE, MATHEW THORTON

MASSACHUSETTS: SAMUAL ADAMS, JOHN ADAMS, JOHN HANCOCK, ROBERT TREAT PAINE, ELBRIDGE GERRY

RHODE ISLAND: STEPHEN HOPKINS, WILLIAN ELLERY

CONNECTICUT: ROGER SHERMAN, SAMUAL HUNTINGTON, WILLIAM WILLIAMS, OLIVER WOLCOTT

NEW YORK: WILLIAM FLOYD, PHILLIP LIVINGSTON, FRANCIS LEWIS, LEWIS MORRIS

NEW JERSEY: RICHARD STOCKTON, JOHN WITHERSPOON, FRANCIS HOPKINSON, JOHN HART, ABRAHAM CLARK

PENNSYLVANIA: ROBERT MORRIS, BENJAMIN RUSH, BENJAMIN FRANKLIN, JOHN MORTON, GEORGE CLYMER, JAMES SMITH, GEORGE TAYLOR, JAMES WILSON, GEORGE ROSS

DELAWARE: GEORGE READ, CEASAR RODNEY, THOMAS MCKEAN

MARYLAND: SAMUAL CHASE, WILLIAM PACA, THOMAS STONE, CHARLES CARROLL OF CARROLLTON

VIRGINIA: GEORGE WYTHE, RICHARD HENRY LEE, THOMAS JEFFERSON, BENJAMINE HARRISON, THOMAS NELSON JR, FRANCIS LIGHTFOOT LEE, CARTER BRAXTON

NORTH CAROLINA: WILLIAM HOOPER, JOSEPH HEWES, JOHN PENN

SOUTH CAROLINA: EDWARD RUTLEDGE, THOMAS HEYWARD JR, THOMAS LYNCH JR, ARTHUR MIDDLETON

GEORGIA: BUTTON GWINNETT, LYMAN HALL, GEORGE WALTON

THE LEE RESOLUTION FOR INDEPENDENCE WAS PASSED BY THE SECOND CONTINENTAL CONGRESS ON JULY 2. THE COMMITTEE OF FIVE DRAFTING THE DECLARATION TO BE READY FOR CONGRESS TO VOTE, JOHN ADAMS PUSHING FOR INDENDENCE PERSUADED THE COMMITTEE TO SELECT THOMAS JEFFERSON TO COMPOSE THE ORIGINAL DRAFT OF THE DOCUMENT. CONGRESS EDITED TO PRODUCE THE FINAL VERSION.

THE DECLARATION WAS A FORMAL EXPLANATION OF WHY CONGRESS HAD VOTED TO DECLARE INDEPENDENCE FROM GREAT BRITAIN. JULY 4 WAS THE DATE THE WORDING WAS APPROVED FOR THE DECLARATION OF INDEPENDENCE.

THE FOUNDING FATHERS WERE A GROUP OF AMERICAN REVOLUTIONARY LEADERS WHO UNITED THE THIRTEEN COLONIES. MOST HISTORIANS AGREE ON A SELECT FEW SUCH AS GEORGE WASHINGTON, BENJAMINE FRANKLIN, JOHN ADAMS, THOMAS JEFFERSON, JAMES MADISON, JOHN JAY, AND ALEXANDER HAMILTON.

CONFEDERACY

THE CONFEDERATE STATES OF AMERICA WAS AN UNRECOGNIZED BREAKAWAY HERRENVOLK REPUBLIC IN NORTH AMERICA THAT EXISTED FROM FEBRUARY 8, 1861 TO MAY 9, 1865. THE CONFEDERACY COMPRISED U.S. STATES THAT DECLARED SUCESSION AND WARRED AGAINST THE UNITED STATES DURING THE AMEICAN CIVIL WAR. THE ELEVEN U.S. STATES WERE:

	READMITTED TO THE UNITED STATES
SOUTH CAROLINA	JULY 9, 1868
MISSISSIPPI	FEBRUARY 23, 1870
FLORIDA	JUNE 25, 1868
ALABAMA	1868
GEORGIA	JULY 15, 1870
LOUISIANA	JULY 9, 1868
TEXAS	1870
VIRGINIA	JANUARY 26, 1870
ARKASAS	JUNE 22, 1868
TENNESSEE	JULY 24, 1866
NORTH CAROLINA	JULY 4, 1868
KENTUCKY	REMAINED NEUTRAL
MISSOURI	JANUARY 16, 1861

PRESIDENT- JEFFERSON DAVIS
VICE PRESIDENT- ALEXANDER STEPHENS
CAPITAL- MONTGOMER ALABAMA UNTIL MAY 29, 1861
RICHMOND VIRGINIA UNTIL APRIL 2-3, 1865
DANVILLE VIRGINIA UNTIL APRIL 10, 1865

About the Author

James R. Bower, retired designer of architectural and mechanical engineering. A U.S. paratrooper, veteran of the 60's and 70's. The president of the Deer Park Art League in Deer Park, Texas.

Bibliography

Wikipedia List of U.S. State and Territory Flowers
https://en.wikipedia.org/wiki/List_of_U.S._state_and_territory_flowers

U.S. State and territory flags
https://en.wikipedia.org/wiki/List_of_flags_of_the_United_States

List of U.S. State Birds
https://en.wikipedia.org/wiki/List_of_U.S._state_birds

Printed in the USA
CPSIA information can be obtained
at www.ICGtesting.com
LVHW050426161124
796806LV00026B/191/J